Keto A Cookb Advanced

Best Keto Air Fryer Recipes for Advanced Users, Super Easy to Prepare and Budget Friendly for Losing Weight in Healthy

Tanya Hackett

Table of Contents

URSULA MAYERT .... Errore. Il segnalibro non è definito.
© COPYRIGHT 2020 BY URSULA MAYERT 7

INTRODUCTION 10

- BLUEBERRY CREAM 14
- BLACKBERRY CHIA JAM 16
- MIXED BERRIES CREAM 18
- AIR FRIED CRUMBED FISH 20
- AIR FRYER MEATLOAF 22
- AIR FRYER SHRIMP A LA BANG 24
- BALSAMIC-GLAZED CARROTS 27
- BAKED POTATOES WITH YOGURT AND CHIVES 29
- BUTTERED BROCCOLI WITH PARMESAN 31
- CREAMY CORN CASSEROLE 33
- CHARRED GREEN BEANS WITH SESAME SEEDS 35
- CINNAMON-SPICED ACORN SQUASH 37
- PARMESAN ASPARAGUS FRIES 39
- CHILI CORN ON THE COB 42
- SPICY CABBAGE 45
- SPICY BROCCOLI WITH HOT SAUCE 47
- CHEESY BROCCOLI GRATIN 49
- AIR FRIED CHICKEN TENDERS 51
- PARMESAN ZUCCHINI CHIPS 53
- CATTLE RANCH GARLIC PRETZELS 55
- HERBY SWEET POTATO CHIPS 57
- CUMIN TORTILLA CHIPS WITH GUACAMOLE 59
- OVEN-DRIED STRAWBERRIES 61
- CHILI CHEESE TOASTS 62
- CHEESE STICKS 64
- BLENDED VEGGIE CHIPS 66
- SWEET APPLE AND PEAR CHIPS 68
- COCOA BANANA CHIPS 70
- CORIANDER ROASTED CHICKPEAS 72
- CORN NUTS 74
- BAKED POTATOES 76
- COCONUT CHICKEN BITES 77
- BUFFALO CAULIFLOWER SNACK 79
- BANANA SNACK 81
- POTATO SPREAD 83
- MEXICAN APPLE SNACK 85
- SHRIMP MUFFINS 87
- ZUCCHINI CAKES 89

CAULIFLOWER BARS 91
PESTO CRACKERS 93
PUMPKIN MUFFINS 95
ZUCCHINI CHIPS 97
BEEF JERKY SNACK 99
HONEY PARTY WINGS 101
SALMON PARTY PATTIES 103
BANANA CHIPS 105
SESAME TOFU CUBES 106
THYME SALTY TOMATOES 108
CREAMY CHICKEN LIVER 110
CATFISH STICKS 112

30-DAY MEAL PLAN 114

CONCLUSION 119

© Copyright 2020 by Tanya Hackett

- All rights reserved.

The following Book is reproduced below with the goal of providing information that is as accurate and reliable as possible. Regardless, purchasing this Book can be seen as consent to the fact that both the publisher and the author of this book are in no way experts on the topics discussed within and that any recommendations or suggestions that are made herein are for entertainment purposes only. Professionals should be consulted as needed prior to undertaking any of the action endorsed herein.

This declaration is deemed fair and valid by both the American Bar Association and the Committee of Publishers Association and is legally binding throughout the United States.

Furthermore, the transmission, duplication, or reproduction of any of the following work including specific information will be considered an illegal act irrespective of if it is done electronically or in print. This extends to creating a secondary or tertiary copy of the work or a recorded copy and is only allowed with the express written consent from the Publisher. All additional right reserved.

The information in the following pages is broadly considered a truthful and accurate account of facts and as such, any inattention, use, or misuse of the information in question by the reader will render any resulting actions solely under their purview. There are no scenarios in which the publisher or the original author of this work can be in any fashion deemed liable for any hardship or damages that may befall them after undertaking information described herein.

Additionally, the information in the following pages is intended only for informational purposes and should thus be thought of as universal. As befitting its nature, it is presented without assurance regarding its prolonged validity or interim quality. Trademarks that are mentioned are done without written consent and can in no way be considered an endorsement from the trademark holder.

Introduction

An air fryer is a relatively new kitchen appliance that has proven to be very popular among consumers. While there are many different varieties available, most air fryers share many common features. They all have heating elements that circulate hot air to cook the food. Most come with pre-programmed settings that assist users in preparing a wide variety of foods.

Air frying is a healthier style of cooking because it uses less oil than traditional deep frying methods. While it preserves the flavor and quality of the food, it reduces the amount of fat used in cooking. Air frying is a common method for "frying" foods that are primarily made with eggs and flour. These foods can be soft or crunchy to your preference by using this method.

How air fryers work

Air fryers use a blower to circulate hot air around food. The hot air heats the moisture on the food until it evaporates and creates steam. As steam builds up around the food, it creates pressure that pulls moisture from the surface of the food and pushes it away from the center, forming small bubbles. The bubbles creates a layer of air that surrounds the food and creates a crispy crust.

Choosing an air fryer

When choosing an air fryer, look for one that has good reviews for customer satisfaction. Start with the features you need, such as power, capacity size and accessories. Look for one that is easy to use. Some air fryers on the market have a built-in timer and adjustable temperature. Look for one with a funnel to catch grease, a basket that is dishwasher-safe and parts that are easy to clean.

How To Use An Air Fryer

For best results, preheat the air fryer at 400 F for 10 minutes. Preheating the air fryer allows it to reach the right temperature faster. In addition, preheating the air fryer is essential to ensure that your food won't burn.

How to cook stuff in an Air Fryer

If you don't have an air fryer yet, you can start playing with your ovens by throwing some frozen fries in there and cooking them until they are browned evenly. Depending on your oven, take a look at the temperature. You may need to increase or decrease the time.

What Foods Can You Cook In An Air Fryer?

Eggs: While you can cook eggs in an air fryer, we don't recommend it because you can't control the cooking time and temperature as precisely as with a traditional frying pan or skillet. It's much easier to get unevenly cooked eggs. You also can't toss in any sauces or seasonings and you won't get crispy, golden brown edges.

Frozen foods: Generally, frozen foods are best cooked in the conventional oven because they need to reach a certain temperature to be properly cooked. The air fryer is not capable of reaching temperatures that result in food being fully cooked.

Dehydrated Foods: Dehydrated foods require deep-frying, which is not something you can do with an air fryer. When it comes to cooking dehydrated foods, the air fryer is not the best option.

Vegetables: You can cook vegetables in an air fryer but you have to make sure that the air fryer is not set at a temperature that will burn them.

To ensure that your vegetables aren't overcooked, start the air fryer with the basket off, then toss in the veggies once the air has heated up and there are no more cold spots.

Make sure to stir the vegetables every few minutes. Cooking them in the basket is also an option, but they may stick together a little bit.

Fries: Frying fries in an air fryer is a good way to get crispy, golden-brown fries without adding lots of oil. Compared to conventional frying, air frying yields fewer calories.

To cook french fries in an air fryer, use a basket or a rack and pour in enough oil to come about halfway up the height of the fries. For best results, make sure the fries are frozen. Turn the air fryer onto 400 degrees and set it for 12 minutes. If you want them extra crispy, you can set it for 18 minutes, but they may burn a bit.

Benefits of an air fryer:

- It's one of the easiest ways to cook healthy foods. Used 4-5 times a week, it's a healthier option than frying with oil in your conventional oven or using canned foods.
- Air fryer meals are an easy way to serve tasty food that doesn't take up lots of space. Air fryers make it possible to cook three times as much food as you can in your microwave.
- Air fryers have a small footprint and you can store them away in a cabinet when not in use.
- They are versatile kitchen appliances. You can use them to cook food for lunch, dinner and snacks.
- Air fryers require little to no fussing in the kitchen. You can use them with the lid on, which means there's less washing up to do.

Blueberry Cream

Preparation Time: 4 minutes

Cooking Time: 20 minutes

Servings: 6

Ingredients:

1. 2cups blueberries
2. Juice of ½ lemon
3. 2tablespoons water
4. 1 teaspoon vanilla extract
5. 2tablespoons swerve

Directions:

- In a large bowl, put all ingredients and mix well.
- Divide this into 6 ramekins, put them in the air fryer and cook at 340 degrees F for 20 minutes

- Cool down and serve.

Nutrition:

Calories: 123

Protein: 3 g.

Fat: 2 g.

Carbs: 4 g.

Blackberry Chia Jam

Preparation Time: 10 minutes

Cooking Time: 30 minutes

Servings: 12

Ingredients:

1. 3cups blackberries
2. ¼ cup swerve
3. 4tablespoons lemon juice
4. 4tablespoons chia seeds

Directions:

- In a pan that suits the air fryer, combine all the Ingredients: and toss.
- Put the pan in the fryer and cook at 300 degrees F for 30 minutes.
- Divide into cups and serve cold.

Nutrition:

Calories: 100
Protein: 1 g.
Fat: 2 g.
Carbs: 3 g.

Mixed Berries Cream

Preparation Time: 5 minutes
Cooking Time: 30 minutes
Servings: 6
Ingredients:

1. 12ounces blackberries
2. 6ounces raspberries
3. 12ounces blueberries
4. ¾ cup swerve
5. 2ounces coconut cream

Directions:

- In a bowl, put all the Ingredients: and mix well.
- Divide this into 6 ramekins, put them in your air fryer and cook at 320 degrees F for 30 minutes.

- Cool down and serve it.

Nutrition:

Calories: 100

Protein: 2 g.

Fat: 1 g.

Carbs: 2 g.

Air Fried Crumbed Fish

Preparation Time: 10 minutes
Cooking Time: 12 minutes
Servings: 4
Ingredients:
　　1. Bread crumbs: 1 cup
　　2. Vegetable oil: ¼ cup
　　3. 4 Flounder fillets
　　4. 1 Beaten egg
　　5. 1 Sliced Lemon

Directions:

- Preheat an air fryer to 350 °F (180 °C).
- In a cup, add the bread crumbs and the oil. Stir until the mixture becomes crumbly and loose.
- Dip the fish fillets in the egg mixture; shake off any excesses. Dip the fillets into a mixture of bread crumbs; until evenly and thoroughly coated.
- Gently lay coated fillets in the preheated air fryer. Cook, about 12 minutes, with a fork, until fish flakes easily. Garnish with sliced lemon.

Nutrition:
Calories: 354 Cal
Fat: 17.7 g
Carbohydrates: 22.5 g
Protein: 26.9 g

Air Fryer Meatloaf

Preparation Time: 10 minutes
Cooking Time: 25 minutes
Servings: 4
Ingredients:

- 1-pound lean beef
- 1 lightly beaten egg
- 3 tablespoons. bread crumbs
- 1 small, finely chopped onion
- 1 tablespoon. chopped fresh thyme
- 1 teaspoon salt
- 1 pinch ground black pepper to taste
- 2 thickly sliced mushrooms
- 1 tablespoon. olive oil

Directions:

- Preheat an air fryer up to 200 degrees C (392 degrees F).
- In a bowl, combine ground beef, egg, bread crumbs, ointment, thyme, salt, and pepper. Knead and mix well.
- Move the mixture of beef into a baking pan and smooth the rim—press chestnuts into the top and coat with olive oil. Place the saucepan in the basket of the air fryer and slide into the air fryer.
- Set 25-minute air fryer timer and roast meatloaf until well browned.

- Set aside the meatloaf for at least 10 minutes before slicing and serving into wedges.

Nutrition:

Calories: 296.8

Protein: 24.8 g

Carbohydrates: 5.9 g

Cholesterol: 125.5 mg

Air Fryer Shrimp a La Bang

Preparation Time: 10 minutes
Cooking Time: 12 minutes
Servings: 2

Ingredients:
1. 1/2 cup mayonnaise
2. 1/4 cup sweet chili sauce
3. 1tablespoon. sriracha sauce
4. 1/4 cup all-purpose flour
5. 1 cup panko bread crumbs
6. Raw shrimp: 1 pound, peeled and deveined
7. 1 leaf lettuce

8. 2green, chopped onions or to taste (optional)

Directions:

- Set temperature of air fryer to 400 degrees F (200 degrees C).
- In a bowl, stir in mayonnaise, chili sauce, and sriracha sauce until smooth. Put some bang sauce, if desired, in a separate bowl for dipping.
- Take a plate and place flour on it. Use a separate plate and place panko bread crumbs on it.
- First coat the shrimp with flour, then mayonnaise mixture, then panko. Place shrimp covered on a baking sheet.
- Place shrimp, without overcrowding, in the air fryer basket.
- Cook for approximately 12 minutes. Repeat with shrimp leftover.
- Use lettuce wraps for serving, garnished with green onion.

Nutrition:

Calories: 415

Fat: 23.9 g

Carbohydrates: 32.7 g

Protein: 23.9 g

Balsamic-Glazed Carrots

Preparation Time: 5 minutes
Cooking Time: 18 minutes
Servings: 3
Ingredients:

1. 3 medium-size carrots, cut into 2-inch × ½-inch sticks
2. 1 tablespoon orange juice
3. 2 teaspoons balsamic vinegar
4. 1 teaspoon maple syrup
5. 1 teaspoon avocado oil
6. ½ teaspoon dried rosemary
7. ¼ teaspoon sea salt
8. ¼ teaspoon lemon zest

Directions:

- Put the carrots in the baking pan and sprinkle with the orange juice, balsamic vinegar, maple syrup, avocado oil, rosemary, sea salt, finished by the lemon zest. Toss well.
- Slide the baking pan into Rack Position 1, select Convection Bake, set temperature to 375°F (190°C), and set time to 18 minutes.
- Stir the carrots several times during the cooking process.

- When cooking is complete, the carrots should be nicely glazed and tender. Remove from the oven and serve hot.

Nutrition:

Calories: 191 Cal

Fat: 6g

Carbohydrates: 31.4g

Protein: 3.7g

Cholesterol: 3mg

Sodium: 447mg

Baked Potatoes with Yogurt and Chives

Preparation Time: 5 minutes
Cooking Time: 35 minutes
Servings: 4
Ingredients:

1. 4(7-ounce / 198-g) russet potatoes, rinsed
2. Olive oil spray
3. ½ teaspoon kosher salt, divided
4. ½ cup 2% plain Greek yogurt
5. ¼ cup minced fresh chives
6. Freshly ground black pepper

Directions:

- Pat the potatoes dry and pierce them all over with a fork. Spritz the potatoes with olive oil spray. Sprinkle with ¼ teaspoon of the salt.

- Transfer the potatoes to the baking pan.

- Slide the baking pan into Rack Position 1, select Convection Bake, set temperature to 400°F (205°C), and set time to 35 minutes.

- When cooking is complete, the potatoes should be fork-tender. Remove from the oven and split open the potatoes. Top with the yogurt, chives, the remaining ¼ teaspoon of salt, and finish with the black pepper. Serve immediately.

Nutrition:

Calories: 172 Cal

Fat: 9.8g

Carbohydrates: 17.5g

Protein: 3.9g

Cholesterol: 84mg

Sodium: 112mg

Buttered Broccoli with Parmesan

Preparation Time: 5 minutes

Cooking Time: 4 minutes

Servings: 4

Ingredients:

1. 1 pound (454 g) broccoli florets
2. 1 medium shallot, minced
3. 2tablespoons olive oil
4. 2tablespoons unsalted butter, melted
5. 2teaspoons minced garlic
6. ¼ cup grated Parmesan cheese

Directions:

- Combine the broccoli florets with the shallot, olive oil, butter, garlic, and Parmesan cheese in a medium bowl and toss until the broccoli florets are thoroughly coated.
- Place the broccoli florets in the baking pan in a single layer.
- Slide the baking pan into Rack Position 1, select Convection Bake, set temperature to 350°F (180°C), and set time to 4 minutes.
- When cooking is complete, the broccoli florets should be crisp-tender. Remove from the oven and serve warm.

Nutrition:

Calories: 191 Cal

Fat: 6g

Carbohydrates: 31.4g

Protein: 3.7g

Cholesterol: 3mg

Sodium: 447mg

Creamy Corn Casserole

Preparation Time: 5 minutes
Cooking Time: 15 minutes
Servings: 4
Ingredients:

1. 2cups frozen yellow corn
2. 1 egg, beaten
3. 3tablespoons flour
4. ½ cup grated Swiss or Havarti cheese
5. ½ cup light cream
6. ¼ cup milk
7. Pinch salt
8. Freshly ground black pepper, to taste
9. 2 tablespoons butter, cut into cubes
10. Nonstick cooking spray

Directions:

- Spritz the baking pan with nonstick cooking spray.
- Stir together the remaining ingredients except the butter in a medium bowl until well incorporated. Transfer the mixture to the prepared baking pan and scatter with the butter cubes.
- Slide the baking pan into Rack Position 1, select Convection Bake, set temperature to 320°F (160°C), and set time to 15 minutes.

- When cooking is complete, the top should be golden brown and a toothpick inserted in the center should come out clean. Remove from the oven. Let the casserole cool for 5 minutes before slicing into wedges and serving.

Nutrition:
Calories: 172 Cal
Fat: 9.8g
Carbohydrates: 17.5g
Protein: 3.9g
Cholesterol: 84mg
Sodium: 112mg

Charred Green Beans with Sesame Seeds

Preparation Time: 5 minutes
Cooking Time: 8 minutes
Servings: 4
Ingredients:

1. 1 tablespoon reduced-sodium soy sauce or tamari
2. ½ tablespoon Sriracha sauce
3. 4teaspoons toasted sesame oil, divided
4. 12ounces (340 g) trimmed green beans
5. ½ tablespoon toasted sesame seeds

Directions:

- Whisk together the soy sauce, Sriracha sauce, and 1 teaspoon of sesame oil in a small bowl until smooth. Set aside.
- Toss the green beans with the remaining sesame oil in a large bowl until evenly coated.
- Place the green beans in the air fryer basket in a single layer.
- Put the air fryer basket on the baking pan and slide into Rack Position 2, select Air Fry, set temperature to 375°F (190°C), and set time to 8 minutes.
- Stir the green beans halfway through the cooking time.

- When cooking is complete, the green beans should be lightly charred and tender. Remove from the oven to a platter. Pour the prepared sauce over the top of green beans and toss well. Serve sprinkled with the toasted sesame seeds.

Nutrition:

Calories: 191 Cal

Fat: 6g

Carbohydrates: 31.4g

Protein: 3.7g

Cholesterol: 3mg

Sodium: 447mg

Cinnamon-Spiced Acorn Squash

Preparation Time: 5 minutes

Cooking Time: 15 minutes

Servings: 2

Ingredients:

1. 1 medium acorn squash, halved crosswise and deseeded
2. 1 teaspoon coconut oil
3. 1 teaspoon light brown sugar
4. Few dashes of ground cinnamon
5. Few dashes of ground nutmeg

Directions:

- On a clean work surface, rub the cut sides of the acorn squash with coconut oil. Scatter with the brown sugar, cinnamon, and nutmeg.
- Put the squash halves in the air fryer basket, cut-side up.
- Put the air fryer basket on the baking pan and slide into Rack Position 2, select Air Fry, set temperature to 325°F (163°C), and set time to 15 minutes.
- When cooking is complete, the squash halves should be just tender when pierced in the center with a paring knife. Remove from the oven. Rest for 5 to 10 minutes and serve warm.

Nutrition:
Calories: 172 Cal
Fat: 9.8g
Carbohydrates: 17.5g
Protein: 3.9g
Cholesterol: 84mg
Sodium: 112mg

Parmesan Asparagus Fries

Preparation Time: 15 minutes
Cooking Time: 6 minutes
Servings: 4
Ingredients:
1. 2egg whites
2. ¼ cup water

3. ¼ cup plus 2 tablespoons grated Parmesan cheese, divided
4. ¾ cup panko bread crumbs
5. ¼ teaspoon salt
6. 12ounces (340 g) fresh asparagus spears, woody ends trimmed
7. Cooking spray

Directions:

- In a shallow dish, whisk together the egg whites and water until slightly foamy. In a separate shallow dish, thoroughly combine ¼ cup of Parmesan cheese, bread crumbs, and salt.

- Dip the asparagus in the egg white, then roll in the cheese mixture to coat well.

- Place the asparagus in the air fryer basket in a single layer, leaving space between each spear. Spritz the asparagus with cooking spray.

- Put the air fryer basket on the baking pan and slide into Rack Position 2, select Air Fry, set temperature to 390°F (199°C), and set time to 6 minutes.

- When cooking is complete, the asparagus should be golden brown and crisp. Remove from the oven. Sprinkle with the remaining 2 tablespoons of cheese and serve hot.

Nutrition:

Calories: 191 Cal
Fat: 6g
Carbohydrates: 31.4g
Protein: 3.7g
Cholesterol: 3mg
Sodium: 447mg

Chili Corn on the Cob

Preparation Time: 10 minutes

Cooking Time: 15 minutes

Servings: 4

Ingredients:

1. 2tablespoon olive oil, divided
2. 2tablespoons grated Parmesan cheese
3. 1 teaspoon garlic powder
4. 1 teaspoon chili powder
5. 1 teaspoon ground cumin
6. 1 teaspoon paprika
7. 1 teaspoon salt
8. ¼ teaspoon cayenne pepper (optional)
9. 4ears fresh corn, shucked

Directions:

- Grease the air fryer basket with 1 tablespoon of olive oil. Set aside.
- Combine the Parmesan cheese, garlic powder, chili powder, cumin, paprika, salt, and cayenne pepper (if desired) in a small bowl and stir to mix well.
- Lightly coat the ears of corn with the remaining 1 tablespoon of olive oil. Rub the cheese mixture all over the ears of corn until completely coated.
- Arrange the ears of corn in the greased basket in a single layer.
- Put the air fryer basket on the baking pan and slide into Rack Position 2, select Air Fry, set temperature to 400°F (205°C), and set time to 15 minutes.
- Flip the ears of corn halfway through the cooking time.
- When cooking is complete, they should be lightly browned. Remove from the oven and let them cool for 5 minutes before serving.

Nutrition:
Calories: 172 Cal
Fat: 9.8g
Carbohydrates: 17.5g
Protein: 3.9g
Cholesterol: 84mg
Sodium: 112mg

Spicy Cabbage

Preparation Time: 5 minutes
Cooking Time: 7 minutes
Servings: 4
Ingredients:
1. 1 head cabbage, sliced into 1-inch-thick ribbons
2. 1 tablespoon olive oil
3. 1 teaspoon garlic powder
4. 1 teaspoon red pepper flakes
5. 1 teaspoon salt
6. 1 teaspoon freshly ground black pepper

Directions:

- Toss the cabbage with the olive oil, garlic powder, red pepper flakes, salt, and pepper in a large mixing bowl until well coated.

- Transfer the cabbage to the baking pan.

- Slide the baking pan into Rack Position 1, select Convection Bake, set temperature to 350°F (180°C), and set time to 7 minutes.

- Flip the cabbage with tongs halfway through the cooking time.

- When cooking is complete, the cabbage should be crisp. Remove from the oven to a plate and serve warm.

Nutrition:

Calories: 172 Cal
Fat: 9.8g
Carbohydrates: 17.5g
Protein: 3.9g
Cholesterol: 84mg
Sodium: 112mg

Spicy Broccoli with Hot Sauce

Preparation Time: 5 minutes

Cooking Time: 14 minutes

Servings: 6

Ingredients:

Broccoli:

1. 1 medium-sized head broccoli, cut into florets
2. 1½ tablespoons olive oil
3. 1 teaspoon shallot powder
4. 1 teaspoon porcini powder
5. ½ teaspoon freshly grated lemon zest
6. ½ teaspoon hot paprika
7. ½ teaspoon granulated garlic

8. ⅓ teaspoon fine sea salt
9. ⅓ teaspoon celery seeds

Hot Sauce:

- ½ cup tomato sauce
- 1 tablespoon balsamic vinegar
- ½ teaspoon ground allspice

Directions:

1. In a mixing bowl, combine all the ingredients for the broccoli and toss to coat. Transfer the broccoli to the air fryer basket.
2. Put the air fryer basket on the baking pan and slide into Rack Position 2, select Air Fry, set temperature to 360°F (182°C), and set time to 14 minutes.
3. Meanwhile, make the hot sauce by whisking together the tomato sauce, balsamic vinegar, and allspice in a small bowl.
4. When cooking is complete, remove the broccoli from the oven and serve with the hot sauce.

Nutrition:

Calories: 191 Cal
Fat: 6g
Carbohydrates: 31.4g
Protein: 3.7g
Cholesterol: 3mg
Sodium: 447mg

Cheesy Broccoli Gratin

Preparation Time: 5 minutes
Cooking Time: 14 minutes
Servings: 2
Ingredients:

- ⅓ cup fat-free milk
- 1 tablespoon all-purpose or gluten-free flour
- ½ tablespoon olive oil
- ½ teaspoon ground sage
- ¼ teaspoon kosher salt
- ⅛ teaspoon freshly ground black pepper
- 2cups roughly chopped broccoli florets
- 6tablespoons shredded Cheddar cheese
- 2tablespoons panko bread crumbs
- 1 tablespoon grated Parmesan cheese
- Olive oil spray

Directions:

1. Spritz the baking pan with olive oil spray.
2. Mix the milk, flour, olive oil, sage, salt, and pepper in a medium bowl and whisk to combine. Stir in the broccoli florets, Cheddar cheese, bread crumbs, and Parmesan cheese and toss to coat.
3. Pour the broccoli mixture into the prepared baking pan.

4. Slide the baking pan into Rack Position 1, select Convection Bake, set temperature to 330°F (166°C), and set time to 14 minutes.

5. When cooking is complete, the top should be golden brown and the broccoli should be tender. Remove from the oven and serve immediately.

Nutrition:

Calories: 172 Cal

Fat: 9.8g

Carbohydrates: 17.5g

Protein: 3.9g

Cholesterol: 84mg

Sodium: 112mg

Air Fried Chicken Tenders

Basic Recipe

Preparation Time: 10 minutes

Cooking Time: 10 minutes

Servings: 4

Ingredients:

1. 1/8 cup flour
2. Pepper and salt to taste
3. Olive spray
4. 1 egg white
5. 12 oz, chicken breasts
6. 1-¼ oz. panko bread crumbs

Directions:

- Trim off excess fat from your chicken breast. Cut into tenders. Season it with pepper and salt. Dip the tenders into flour and after that into egg whites and bread crumbs. Keep in the fryer basket. Apply olive spray and cook for 10 minutes at 350 degrees F. Serve.

Nutrition:

Calories 399

Carbs 18g

Fat 11g

Protein 57g

Parmesan Zucchini Chips

Basic Recipe

Preparation Time: 15 minutes

Cooking Time: 10 minutes

Servings: 4

Ingredients:

1. Salt to taste
2. 3 medium zucchinis
3. 1 cup grated Parmesan cheese

Directions:

- Preheat the oven in Air Fryer mode at 110 F for 2 to 3 minutes Use a mandolin slicer to very finely slice the zucchinis, season with salt, and coat well with the Parmesan cheese. In batches, arrange as lots of zucchini pieces as possible in a single layer on the cooking tray. When the device is ready, move the cooking tray onto the leading rack of the oven and close the oven. Set the timer to 7 minutes and press Start. Cook till the cheese melts while turning the midway. Transfer the chips to serving bowls to cool and make the remaining. Serve warm.

Nutrition:

Calories 107

Fat 6.99 g

Carbs 3.73 g

Protein 7.33 g

Cattle Ranch Garlic Pretzels

Basic Recipe

Preparation Time: 10 minutes

Cooking Time: 15 minutes

Servings: 4

Ingredients:

1. ½ tsp garlic powder
2. 2 cups pretzels
3. 1 ½ tsp ranch dressing mix
4. 1 tbsp melted butter

Directions:

- Preheat the oven in Air Fryer mode at 270 F for 2 to 3 minutes. In a medium bowl, blend all the ingredients up until well-integrated, pour into the rotisserie basket and near to seal. Repair the basket onto the lever in the oven and close the oven. Set the timer to 15 minutes, press Start and cook until the pretzels are gently browner. After, open the oven, secure the basket utilizing the rotisserie lift and transfer the snack into serving bowls. Permit cooling and delight in.

Nutrition:

Calories 35

Fat 3.72 g

Carbs 0.4 g

Protein 0.12 g

Herby Sweet Potato Chips

Basic Recipe

Preparation Time: 10 minutes

Cooking Time: 10 minutes

Servings: 4

Ingredients:

1. 1 tsp dried mixed herbs
2. 2 medium sweet potatoes, peeled
3. 1 tbsp olive oil

Directions:

- Pre-heat the oven in Air Fry mode at 375 F for 2 to 3 minutes. On the other hand, utilize a mandolin slicer to thinly slice the sweet potatoes, transfer to a medium bowl and blend well with the herbs and olive oil till well coated. In batches, organize as numerous sweet potato pieces as possible in a single layer on the cooking tray. When the device is ready, slide the cooking tray onto the top rack of the oven and close the oven. Set the timer to 7 minutes and press Start. Cook till the sweet potatoes are crispy while turning midway. Transfer the chips to serving bowls when prepared and make the remaining in the same manner. Delight in.

Nutrition:

Calories 87

Fat 3.48 g

Carbs 13.38 g
Protein 1.03 g

Cumin Tortilla Chips with Guacamole

Basic Recipe

Preparation Time: 5 minutes

Cooking Time: 15 minutes

Servings: 4

Ingredients:
1. For the tortilla chips:
2. 2 tablespoon olive oil
3. 12 corn tortillas
4. 1 tbsp paprika powder
5. 1 tbsp cumin powder
6. Salt and black pepper to taste

7. For the guacamole:
8. 1 little company tomato, sliced
9. A pinch dried parsley
10. 1 big avocado, pitted and peeled

Directions:

- Preheat the oven in Air Fry mode at 375 F for 2 to 3 minutes in a medium bowl, mix all the ingredients for the tortilla chips well and put the mix into the rotisserie basket.
- Close to seal. Fix the basket onto the lever in the oven and close the oven. Set the timer to 15 minutes, press Start and cook until the tortillas are golden brown.
- After, open the oven, take out the basket using the rotisserie lift and transfer the chips to serving bowls.Meanwhile, as the chips cooked, in a little bowl, mash the avocados and blend with the tomato and parsley up until well combined.
- Serve the tortilla chips with the guacamole.

Nutrition:

Calories 159
Fat 14.74 g
Carbs 7.82 g
Protein 1.94 g

Oven-Dried Strawberries

Basic Recipe
Preparation Time: 10 minutes
Cooking Time: 10 minutes
Servings: 4
Ingredients:
1. 1-poundlarge strawberries

Directions:
- Pre-heat the air fryer in Dehydrate mode at 110 F for 2 to 3 minutes Use a mandolin slicer to thinly slice the strawberries. In batches, arrange a few of the strawberry pieces in a single layer on the cooking tray.
- When the device is ready, move the cooking tray onto the top rack of the oven and close the oven
- Set the timer to 7 minutes and press Start. Cook until the fruits are crispy.
- Transfer the fruit chips to serving bowls when all set and make the remaining in the same manner. Delight in.

Nutrition:
Calories 36
Fat 0.34 g
Carbs 8.71 g
Protein 0.76 g

Chili Cheese Toasts

Basic Recipe
Preparation Time: 5 minutes
Cooking Time: 10 minutes
Servings: 4
Ingredients:

2. 1 tsp garlic powder
3. 1 tsp red chili flakes
4. 6 pieces sandwich bread
5. 4 tablespoon butter
6. 1 cup grated cheddar cheese
7. 2 little fresh red chilies, deseeded and minced
8. ½ tsp salt
9. 1 tablespoon sliced fresh parsley

Directions:

1. Pre-heat the oven in Broil mode at 375 F for 2 to 3 minutes Spread the butter on one side of each bread pieces and lay on a tidy, flat surface.
2. Divide the cheddar cheese on top and followed with the remaining ingredients. Lay 3 pieces of the bread on the cooking tray, slide the tray onto the middle rack of the oven, and close the oven. Set the timer for 3 to 4 minutes and press Start.

3. Cook till the cheese melts and is golden brown on top. Remove the first batch when ready and prepare the other three bread pieces. Slice them into triangle halves and serve immediately.

Nutrition:

Calories 105

Fat 11.53 g

Carbs 0.68 g

Protein 0.29 g

Cheese Sticks

Basic Recipe

Preparation Time: 10 minutes

Cooking Time: 10 minutes

Servings: 6

Ingredients:

- 1 teaspoon garlic powder
- 1 teaspoon of Italian spices
- ¼ teaspoon rosemary, ground
- 2 eggs
- 1 cheese sticks
- ¼ cup parmesan cheese, grated
- ¼ cup whole-wheat flour

Directions:

1. Unwraps the cheese sticks. Keep aside. Beat the eggs into a bowl. Mix the cheese, flavorings, and flour in another bowl. Now roll the sticks in the egg and then into the batter. Coat well. Keep them in your air fryer basket. Cook for 7 minutes at 370 degrees F. Serve hot.

Nutrition:

Calories 76

Carbs 5g

Fat 4g

Protein 5g

Blended Veggie Chips

Basic Recipe
Preparation Time: 20 minutes
Cooking Time: 10 minutes
Servings: 4
Ingredients:
- 1 big carrot
- 1 tsp salt
- 1 tsp Italian spices
- 1 zucchini
- 1 sweet potato peeled
- ½ tsp pepper
- 1 red beet, peeled
- A pinch cumin powders

Directions:
1. Preheat the air fryer in Dehydrate mode at 110 F for 2 to 3 minutes
2. Utilize a mandolin slicer to thinly slice all the vegetables and transfer to a medium bowl. Season it with salt, Italian spices, and cumin powder. In batches, organize some of the veggies in a single layer on the cooking tray.

3. When the device is ready, move the cooking tray onto the top rack of the oven and close the oven then set the timer to 7 or 9 minutes and press Start. Cook up until the veggies are crispy. Transfer the vegetables to serving bowls when all set and make the staying in the same manner. Delight in.

Nutrition:

Calories 84

Fat 0.15 g

Carbs 18.88 g

Protein 2.25 g

Sweet Apple and Pear Chips

Basic Recipe
Preparation Time: 15 minutes
Cooking Time: 10 minutes
Servings: 4
Ingredients:
- 6 pears, peeled
- 6 Honey crisp apples

Directions:
1. Pre-heat the air fryer in Dehydrate mode at 110 F for 2 to 3 minutes. On the other hand, utilize a mandolin slicer to very finely slice the apples and pears. In batches, set up a few of the fruit slices in a single layer on the cooking tray.
2. When the device is ready, move the cooking tray onto the top rack of the oven and close the oven
3. Set the timer to 7 minutes and press Start. Cook till the fruits are crispy. Transfer the fruit chips to serving bowls when all set and make the staying in the same manner. Take pleasure in.

Nutrition:
Calories 142
Fat 0.46 g
Carbs 37.7g
Protein 0.71g

Cocoa Banana Chips

Basic Recipe
Preparation Time: 5 minutes
Cooking Time: 7 minutes
Servings: 4
Ingredients:
- ¼ tsp cocoa powder
- 5 large firm bananas, peeled
- A pinch of cinnamon powder

Directions:

1. Preheat the air fryer in Dehydrate mode at 110 F for 2 to 3 minutes. On the other hand, utilize a mandolin slicer to very finely slice the bananas, and coat well with the cocoa powder and the cinnamon powder. In batches, organize as many banana pieces as possible in a single layer on the cooking tray.
2. When the device is ready, slide the cooking tray onto the top rack of the oven and close the oven set the timer to 7 minutes and press Start. Cook until the banana pieces are crispy. Transfer the chips to serving bowls when all set and make the remaining in the same manner. Take pleasure in.

Nutrition:

Calories 152

Fat 0.57 g

Carbs 38.89 g

Protein 1.87 g

Coriander Roasted Chickpeas

Basic Recipe
Preparation Time: 10 minutes
Cooking Time: 45minutes
Servings: 2
Ingredients:

- ¼ tsp garlic powder
- 1 (15 oz) can chickpeas, Dry-out pipes
- ¼ tsp ground coriander
- 1/8 tsp salt
- ¼ tsp chili pepper powder
- ¼ tsp curry powder
- ¼ tsp ground cumin
- ¼ tsp paprika
- Olive oil for spraying

Directions:

1. Pre-heat the oven in Air Fryer mode at 375 F for 2 to 3 minutes in a medium bowl, mix the chickpeas with all the spices until well-integrated and pour into the rotisserie basket. Grease lightly with olive oil, shake the basket, and close the seal.

2. Fix the basket onto the lever in the oven and close the oven. Set the timer to 35 or 45 minutes, press Start and cook up until the chickpeas are golden brown. After, open the oven, take out the basket utilizing the rotisserie lift and transfer the treat into serving bowls. Allow cooling and delight in.

Nutrition:

Calories 91

Fat 1.82 g

Carbs 14.87 g

Protein 4.61 g

Corn Nuts

Basic Recipe

Preparation Time: 10 minutes

Cooking Time: 20 minutes

Servings: 8

Ingredients:

1. 3 tablespoons of vegetable oil
2. 1 oz. white corn
3. 1-½ teaspoons salt

Directions:

3. Cover the corn with water in a bowl. Keep aside. Dry out the corn. Spread it on a flat pan and use paper towels to pat dry.

4. Pre-heat your air fryer to 400 degrees F. Transfer the corn to a bowl then include salt and oil. Stir to coat uniformly.
5. Keep the corn in your air fryer basket. Cook for 8 minutes Shake the basket and cook for 10 minutes more. Transfer to a plate lined with a paper towel. Set aside to cool.

Nutrition:

Calories 240

Fat 8g

Carbs 36g

Protein 6g

Baked Potatoes

Intermediate Recipe

Preparation Time: 10 minutes

Cooking Time: 1hour

Servings: 2

Ingredients:

- ½ teaspoon of coarse sea salt
- 1 tablespoon peanut oil
- 2 large potatoes, scrubbed

Directions:

1. Pre-heat your air fryer to 400 degrees F. Brush peanut oil on your potatoes and sprinkle some salt. Then keep them in the basket of your air fryer.
2. Cook the potatoes for an hour. Serve hot.

Nutrition:

Calories 360

Carbs 64g

Fat 8g

Protein 8g

Coconut Chicken Bites

Basic Recipe

Preparation Time: 10 minutes

Cooking Time: 15 minutes

Servings: 4

Ingredients:

- 2 teaspoons garlic powder
- 2 eggs
- Salt and black pepper to the taste
- ¾ cup panko bread crumbs
- ¾ cup coconut, shredded
- Cooking spray
- 8 chicken tenders

Directions:

1. Using a bucket, mix pepper, salt and eggs with garlic powder and whisk well.
2. In another bowl, mix coconut with panko and stir well.
3. Dip the chicken tenders in eggs mix and then coat in coconut one well.
4. Spray chicken bites with cooking spray, place them in your air fryer's basket and cook them at 350 degrees F for 10 minutes
5. Serve.
6. Enjoy!

Nutrition:

Calories 252
Fat 4
Carbs 14
Protein 24

Buffalo Cauliflower Snack

Basic Recipe
Preparation Time: 10 minutes
Cooking Time: 15 minutes
Servings: 4
Ingredients:

- 4 cups cauliflower florets
- 1 cup panko bread crumbs
- ¼ cup butter, melted

- ¼ cup buffalo sauce
- Mayonnaise for serving

Directions:

- In a bowl, mix the buffalo sauce and butter and beat well. Soak cauliflower florets in this mix and coat with breadcrumbs. Put them in the air fryer basket and cook at 350 degrees Fahrenheit for 15 minutes. Arrange them on a platter and serve with mayo on the side. Enjoy!

Nutrition:

Calories 241

Fat 4

Carbs 8

Protein 4

Banana Snack

Basic Recipe

Preparation Time: 10 minutes

Cooking Time: 5 minutes

Servings: 8

Ingredients:
1. 16 baking cups crust
2. ¼ cup peanut butter
3. ¾ cup chocolate chips
4. 1 banana, peeled and sliced into 16 pieces
5. 1 tablespoon vegetable oil

Directions:
1. Put chocolate chips in a small pot, heat up over low heat, stir until it melts and take off heat.
2. In a bowl, mix peanut butter with coconut oil and whisk well.
3. Spoon 1 teaspoon chocolates mix in a cup, add 1 banana slice and top with 1 teaspoon butter mix
4. Repeat with the rest of the cups, place them all into a dish that fits your air fryer, cook at 320 degrees F for 5 minutes, transfer to a freezer and keep there until you serve them as a snack.

Enjoy!

Nutrition:

Calories 70

Fat 4
Carbs 10
Protein 1

Potato Spread

Basic Recipe
Preparation Time: 10 minutes
Cooking Time: 10 minutes
Servings: 10
Ingredients:

- 19 ounces canned garbanzo beans, Dried
- 1 cup sweet potatoes, peeled and chopped
- ¼ cup tahini
- 2 tablespoons lemon juice
- 1 tablespoon olive oil
- 5 garlic cloves, minced
- ½ teaspoon cumin, ground
- 2 tablespoons water
- A pinch of salt and white pepper

Directions:

1. Put potatoes in your air fryer's basket, cook them at 360 degrees F for 15 minutes, cool them down, peel, put them in your food processor and pulse well. Basket, add sesame paste, garlic, beans, lemon juice, cumin, water and oil and pulse really well. Add salt and pepper, pulse again, divide into bowls and serve.

Enjoy!
Nutrition:
Calories 200

Fat 3
Carbs 20
Protein 11

Mexican Apple Snack

Basic Recipe
Preparation Time: 10 minutes
Cooking Time: 5 minutes
Servings: 4
Ingredients:

- 3 big apples, cored, peeled and cubed
- 2 teaspoons lemon juice
- ¼ cup pecans, chopped
- ½ cup dark chocolate chips
- ½ cup clean caramel sauce

Directions:

1. In a bowl, mix apples with lemon juice, stir and transfer to a pan that fits your air fryer.
2. Add chocolate chips, pecans, Drizzle with the caramel sauce, toss, introduce in your air fryer and cook at 320 degrees F for 5 minutes
3. Toss gently, divide into small bowls and serve right away as a snack.
4. Enjoy!

Nutrition:

Calories 200

Fat 4

Carbs 20

Protein 3

Shrimp Muffins

Basic Recipe

Preparation Time: 10 minutes

Cooking Time: 26minutes

Servings: 6

Ingredients:

- 1 spaghetti squash, peeled and halved
- 2 tablespoons mayonnaise
- 1 cup mozzarella, shredded
- 8 ounces shrimp, peeled, cooked and chopped
- 1 and ½ cups panko
- 1 teaspoon parsley flakes
- 1 garlic clove, minced
- Salt and black pepper to the taste

- Cooking spray

Directions:

1. Put squash halves in your air fryer, cook at 350 degrees F for 16 minutes, leave aside to cool down and scrape flesh into a bowl. Add salt, pepper, parsley flakes, panko, shrimp, mayo and mozzarella and stir well.
2. Spray a muffin tray that fits your air fryer with cooking spray and divide squash and shrimp mix in each cup. Introduce in the fryer and cook at 360 degrees F for 10 minutes
3. Arrange muffins on a platter and serve as a snack.
4. Enjoy!

Nutrition:

Calories 60

Fat 2g

Carbs 4g

Protein 4g

Zucchini Cakes

Basic Recipe
Preparation Time: 10 minutes
Cooking Time: 12 minutes
Servings: 8

Ingredients:

- Cooking spray
- ½ cup dill, chopped
- 1 egg
- ½ cup whole wheat flour
- Salt and black pepper to the taste
- 1 yellow onion, chopped
- 2 garlic cloves, minced
- 3 zucchinis, grated

Directions:

1. In a bowl, mix zucchinis with garlic, onion, flour, salt, pepper, egg and dill, stir well, shape small patties out of this mix, spray them with cooking spray, place them in the air fryer's basket and boil at 370 degrees F for 6 minutes on each side.
2. Serve them as a snack right away.
3. Enjoy!

Nutrition:

Calories 60

Fat 1g

Carbs 6g
Protein 2g

Cauliflower Bars

Basic Recipe

Preparation Time: 10 minutes

Cooking Time: 25 minutes

Servings: 12

Ingredients:

- 1 big cauliflower head, florets separated
- ½ cup mozzarella, shredded
- ¼ cup egg whites
- 1 teaspoon Italian seasoning
- Salt and black pepper to the taste

Directions:

1. Put cauliflower florets in your food processor, pulse well, spread on a lined baking sheet that fits your air fryer, introduce in the fryer and cook at 360 degrees F for 10 minutes
2. Transfer cauliflower to a bowl, add salt, pepper, cheese, egg whites and Italian seasoning, stir really well, spread this into a rectangle pan that fits your air fryer, press well, introduce in the fryer and cook at 360 degrees F for 15 minutes more. Cut into 12 bars, arrange them on a platter and serve as a snack
3. Enjoy!

Nutrition:

Calories 50

Fat 1g

Carbs 3g

Protein 3 g

Pesto Crackers

Basic Recipe

Preparation Time: 10 minutes

Cooking Time: 17 minutes

Servings: 6

Ingredients:

- ½ teaspoon baking powder
- Salt and black pepper to the taste
- 1 and ¼ cups flour
- ¼ teaspoon basil, dried
- 1 garlic clove, minced
- 2 tablespoons basil pesto
- 3 tablespoons butter

Directions:

1. In a bowl, mix salt, pepper, baking powder, flour, garlic, cayenne, basil, pesto and butter and stir until you obtain a dough.
2. Spread this dough on a lined baking sheet that fits your air fryer, introduce in the fryer at 325 degrees F and Bake it for 17 minutes
3. Leave aside to cool down, cut crackers and serve them as a snack.
4. Enjoy!

Nutrition:

Calories 200

Fat 20

Carbs 4

Protein 7

Pumpkin Muffins

Basic Recipe
Preparation Time: 10 minutes
Cooking Time: 15 minutes
Servings: 8
Ingredients:

- ¼ cup butter
- ¾ cup pumpkin puree
- 2 tablespoons flaxseed meal
- ¼ cup flour
- ½ cup sugar
- ½ teaspoon nutmeg, ground
- 1 teaspoon cinnamon powder
- ½ teaspoon baking soda
- 1 egg
- ½ teaspoon baking powder

Directions:

1. In a bowl, mix butter with pumpkin puree and egg and blend well.
2. Add flaxseed meal, flour, sugar, baking soda, baking powder, nutmeg and cinnamon and stir well.
3. Spoon this into a muffin pan that fits your fryer introduces in the fryer at 350 degrees F and Bake it for 15 minutes
4. Serve muffins cold as a snack.

5. Enjoy!

Nutrition:

Calories 50

Fat 3

Carbs 2

Protein 2

Zucchini Chips

Basic Recipe

Preparation Time: 10 minutes

Cooking Time: 1hour

Servings: 6

Ingredients:

- 3 zucchinis, thinly sliced
- Salt and black pepper to the taste
- 2 tablespoons olive oil
- 2 tablespoons balsamic vinegar

Directions:

1. Using a bucket, mix vinegar with oil adding pepper with salt and stir well.

2. Add zucchini slices, toss to coat well, introduce in your air fryer and cook at 200 degrees F for 1 hour.
3. Serve zucchini chips cold as a snack.
4. Enjoy!

Nutrition:

Calories 40

Fat 3

Carbs 3

Protein 7

Beef Jerky Snack

Intermediate Recipe
Preparation Time: 2 hours
Cooking Time: 1hour and 30 minutes
Servings: 6
Ingredients:

- 2 cups soy sauce
- ½ cup Worcestershire sauce
- 2 tablespoons black peppercorns
- 2 tablespoons black pepper
- 2 pounds beef round, sliced

Directions:

1. In a bowl, mix soy sauce with black peppercorns, black pepper and Worcestershire sauce and whisk well.
2. Add beef slices, toss to coat and leave aside in the fridge for 6 hours.
3. Introduce beef rounds in your air fryer and cook them at 370 degrees F for 1 hour and 30 minutes
4. Transfer to a bowl and serve cold.
5. Enjoy!

Nutrition:

Calories 300

Fat 12

Carbs 3

Protein 8 g

Honey Party Wings

Intermediate Recipe

Preparation Time: 1hour and 12 minutes

Cooking Time: 10 minutes

Servings: 8

Ingredients:

- 16 chicken wings
- 2 tablespoons soy sauce
- 2 tablespoons of honey
- Salt and black pepper taste to taste
- 2 tablespoons lime juice

Directions:

1. In a bowl, mix the wings with soy sauce, honey, salt, pepper and lime juice, mix well and put in the refrigerator for 1 hour. Transfer the wings to an air fryer, cook at 360 degrees F for 12 minutes, and turn it over halfway.
2. Serve on a plate and serve as an appetizer. Enjoy!

Nutrition:

Calories 211

Fat 4

Carbs 14

Protein 3

Salmon Party Patties

Basic Recipe
Preparation Time: 10 minutes
Cooking Time: 22 minutes
Servings: 4
Ingredients:

- 3 big potatoes, boiled, Dried and mashed
- 1 big salmon fillet, skinless, boneless
- 2 tablespoons parsley, chopped
- 2 tablespoon dill, chopped
- Salt and black pepper to the taste
- 1 egg
- 2 tablespoons bread crumbs
- Cooking spray

Directions:

1. Place salmon in your air fryer's basket and cook for 10 minutes at 360 degrees F.
2. Transfer salmon to a cutting board, cool it down, flake it and put it in a bowl.

3. Add mashed potatoes, salt, pepper, dill, parsley, egg and bread crumbs, stir well and shape 8 patties out of this mix. Place salmon patties in your air fryer's basket, spry them with cooking oil, and for 12 minutes cook at 360 degrees F, flipping them halfway, transfer them to a platter and serve as an appetizer. Enjoy!

Nutrition:

Calories 231

Fat 3

Carbs 14

Protein 4

Banana Chips

Basic Recipe
Preparation Time: 10 minutes
Cooking Time: 15 minutes
Servings: 4
Ingredients:
4 bananas, peeled and sliced
A pinch of salt
½ teaspoon turmeric powder
½ teaspoon chaat masala
1 teaspoon olive oil
Directions:

- In a bowl, mix banana slices with salt, turmeric, chaat masala and oil, toss and leave aside for 10 minutes Transfer banana slices to your preheated air fryer at 360 degrees F and cook them for 15 minutes flipping them once.
- Serve as a snack.
- Enjoy!

Nutrition:
Calories 121
Fat 1
Carbs 3
Protein 3

Sesame Tofu Cubes

Basic Recipe

Preparation Time: 20 minutes

Cooking Time: 20 minutes

Servings: 2

Ingredients:

1. 8 oz tofu
2. 1 teaspoon cornstarch
3. 1 teaspoon scallions, chopped
4. 1 teaspoon rice vinegar
5. 1 teaspoon sesame oil
6. 1 teaspoon soy sauce

Directions:

- Cut the tofu into the cubes.
- Put the tofu cubes in the bowl and sprinkle with the rice vinegar, sesame oil, and soy sauce.
- Shake the mixture.
- Leave the tofu for 10 minutes to marinate.
- Preheat the air fryer to 370 F.
- Sprinkle the marinated tofu with the cornstarch and put in the air fryer basket.
- Cook tofu for 20 minutes
- Shake the tofu after 11 minutes of cooking.
- Then chill the tofu gently and sprinkle with the chopped scallions.
- Enjoy!

Nutrition:

Calories 108

Fat 7

Carbs 3.4

Protein 9.5

Thyme Salty Tomatoes

Basic Recipe

Preparation Time: 10 minutes

Cooking Time: 10 minutes

Servings: 2

Ingredients:

1. 2 tomatoes
2. 1 tablespoon thyme
3. 1 pinch salt
4. 1 teaspoon olive oil

Directions:

- Preheat the air fryer to 375 F.
- Slice the tomatoes.
- Then combine together thyme and salt. Shake the mixture.
- Sprinkle the sliced tomatoes with the thyme mixture. Place the sliced tomatoes in the air fryer and spray with the olive oil.
- Cook the tomatoes for 10 minutes
- When the tomatoes are cooked: they should have tender and little bit dry texture.
- Enjoy!

Nutrition:

Calories 46

Fat 2.7

Carbs 5.6
Protein 1.2

Creamy Chicken Liver

Basic Recipe

Preparation Time: 10 minutes

Cooking Time: 10 minutes

Servings: 2

Ingredients:

1. 7 oz chicken liver
2. ¼ cup water
3. 1 tablespoon butter
4. 2 teaspoon cream
5. 1 tablespoon fresh dill, chopped
6. 1 pinch salt

Directions:

- Preheat the air fryer to 390 F.
- Combine together water, chicken liver, and salt.
- Mix the mixture and place it in the air fryer basket.
- Cook the chicken liver for 10 minutes
- Stir it after 5 minutes of cooking.
- Then transfer the cooked chicken liver to the bowl.
- Add cream and butter.
- Blend the mixture until smooth.
- After this, add chopped fresh dill and stir gently.
- Serve the meal and enjoy!

Nutrition:

Calories 223

Fat 12.5
Carbs 1.9
Protein 24

Catfish Sticks

Basic Recipe

Preparation Time: 10 minutes

Cooking Time: 10 minutes

Servings: 2

Ingredients:

1. 8 oz catfish fillet
2. ½ teaspoon salt
3. ½ teaspoon ground black pepper
4. ¼ cup panko breadcrumbs
5. 1 egg
6. ½ teaspoon olive oil

Directions:

- Cut the catfish fillet into 2 medium pieces (sticks).
- Then sprinkle the catfish with the salt and ground black pepper.
- Beat the egg in the bowl and whisk it.
- Dip the catfish fillets in the whisked egg.
- After this, coat the fish in the panko breadcrumbs.
- Preheat the air fryer to 380 F.
- Put the fish sticks in the air fryer basket and spray with the olive oil.
- Cook the fish sticks for 10 minutes
- Flip the sticks into another side after 10 minutes of cooking.

- When the fish sticks are cooked: let them chill gently.
- Serve the meal!

Nutrition:

Calories 231

Fat 12.2

Carbs 8

Protein 21.5

30-Day Meal Plan

Day	Breakfast	Lunch/dinner	Dessert
1	Shrimp Skillet	Spinach Rolls	Matcha Crepe Cake
2	Coconut Yogurt with Chia Seeds	Goat Cheese Fold-Overs	Pumpkin Spices Mini Pies
3	Chia Pudding	Crepe Pie	Nut Bars
4	Egg Fat Bombs	Coconut Soup	Pound Cake
5	Morning "Grits"	Fish Tacos	Tortilla Chips with Cinnamon Recipe
6	Scotch Eggs	Cobb Salad	Granola Yogurt with Berries
7	Bacon Sandwich	Cheese Soup	Berry Sorbet
8	Noatmeal	Tuna Tartare	Coconut Berry Smoothie
9	Breakfast Bake with Meat	Clam Chowder	Coconut Milk Banana Smoothie

10	Breakfast Bagel	Asian Beef Salad	Mango Pineapple Smoothie
11	Egg and Vegetable Hash	Keto Carbonara	Raspberry Green Smoothie
12	Cowboy Skillet	Cauliflower Soup with Seeds	Loaded Berries Smoothie
13	Feta Quiche	Prosciutto-Wrapped Asparagus	Papaya Banana and Kale Smoothie
14	Bacon Pancakes	Stuffed Bell Peppers	Green Orange Smoothie
15	Waffles	Stuffed Eggplants with Goat Cheese	Double Berries Smoothie
16	Chocolate Shake	Korma Curry	Energizing Protein Bars
17	Eggs in Portobello Mushroom Hats	Zucchini Bars	Sweet and Nutty Brownies
18	Matcha Fat Bombs	Mushroom Soup	Keto Macho Nachos

19	Keto Smoothie Bowl	Stuffed Portobello Mushrooms	Peanut Butter Choco Banana Gelato with Mint
20	Salmon Omelet	Lettuce Salad	Cinnamon Peaches and Yogurt
21	Hash Brown	Onion Soup	Pear Mint Honey Popsicles
22	Black's Bangin' Casserole	Asparagus Salad	Orange and Peaches Smoothie
23	Bacon Cups	Cauliflower Tabbouleh	Coconut Spiced Apple Smoothie
24	Spinach Eggs and Cheese	Beef Salpicao	Sweet and Nutty Smoothie
25	Taco Wraps	Stuffed Artichoke	Ginger Berry Smoothie
26	Coffee Donuts	Spinach Rolls	Vegetarian Friendly Smoothie
27	Egg Baked Omelet	Goat Cheese Fold-Overs	ChocNut Smoothie
28	Ranch Risotto	Crepe Pie	Coco Strawberry Smoothie

29	Scotch Eggs	Coconut Soup	Egg Spinach Berries Smoothie
30	Fried Eggs	Fish Tacos	Creamy Dessert Smoothie

Conclusion

Thanks for making it to the end of this book. An air fryer is a relatively new addition to the kitchen, and it's easy to see why people are getting excited about using it. With an air fryer, you can make crispy fries, chicken wings, chicken breasts and steaks in minutes. There are many delicious foods that you can prepare without adding oil or grease to your meal. Again make sure to read the instructions on your air fryer and follow the rules for proper usage and maintenance. Once your air fryer is in good working condition, you can really get creative and start experimenting your way to healthy food that tastes great.

That's it! Thank you!

CPSIA information can be obtained
at www.ICGtesting.com
Printed in the USA
LVHW082103030521
686351LV00010B/463